Easy Baby Knits

Unique Patterns for Your Little Ones

By

Vickie I Fuller

THIS BOOK

BELONGS TO

....

....

With so many books out there to choose from, I want to thank you for choosing this one and taking precious time out of your life to buy and read my work. Readers like you are the reason I take such passion in creating these books.

It is with gratitude and humility that I express how honored I am to become a part of your life and I hope that you take the same pleasure in reading this book as I did in writing it.

Can I ask one small favour? I ask that you write an honest and open review on Amazon of what you thought of the book. This will help other readers make an informed choice on whether to buy this book.

My sincerest thanks.

Table of Contents

SUMMARY

Celebrating the Joys of Parenthood and Knitting: Parenthood is a beautiful journey filled with countless joys and precious moments. From the first time you hold your baby in your arms to watching them take their first steps, every milestone is a cause for celebration. And what better way to commemorate these special moments than through the art of knitting?

Knitting, a timeless craft that has been passed down through generations, allows parents to create unique and meaningful items for their little ones. From cozy blankets and adorable hats to cute booties and soft toys, the possibilities are endless. Each stitch is infused with love and care, making these handmade creations even more special.

The act of knitting itself is a therapeutic and calming experience. As parents, we often find ourselves caught up in the hustle and bustle of daily life, juggling work, household chores, and the demands of raising a child. Knitting provides a much-needed escape, allowing us to slow down, focus on the present moment, and channel our creativity into something tangible.

Moreover, knitting offers a sense of accomplishment and pride. As we see our projects take shape, stitch by stitch, we feel a deep satisfaction knowing that we are creating something beautiful and meaningful for our children. It is a way to express our love and devotion, and to provide them with something that is truly one-of-a-kind.

Beyond the tangible items, knitting also fosters a sense of connection and community. Joining knitting groups or attending knitting circles allows parents to meet like-minded individuals who share their passion for both parenthood and knitting. These gatherings provide a space for sharing stories, tips, and patterns, as well as offering support and encouragement. It is a chance to bond with others who understand the joys and challenges of raising children while pursuing a creative outlet.

Furthermore, knitting can be a wonderful way to teach our children about patience, perseverance, and the value of handmade items. In a world where everything is readily available and disposable, knitting teaches them the importance of craftsmanship and the satisfaction that comes from creating something with their own hands. It instills in them a sense of pride and appreciation for the time and effort that goes into making something truly special.

In conclusion, celebrating the joys of parenthood and knitting go hand in hand. Knitting allows parents to create unique and meaningful items for their children, while also providing a therapeutic and calming experience. It fosters a sense of connection and community, and teaches valuable life lessons to both parents and children.

The Significance and Sentimentality of Handmade Baby Items of Knitting: Handmade baby items of knitting hold a significant place in the hearts of parents and caregivers alike. These meticulously crafted pieces not only provide warmth and comfort to newborns but also carry a deep sentimental value that cannot be replicated by store-bought items.

The act of knitting itself is a labor of love. Each stitch is carefully thought out and executed, resulting in a unique and one-of-a-kind creation. The time and effort put into making these items make them all the more special. Knitters often pour their heart and soul into their work, infusing it with their love and care for the baby who will eventually wear or use the item.

Furthermore, handmade baby items of knitting often become cherished heirlooms that are passed down from one generation to another. These items hold a rich history and carry the memories of the person who made them. They become a tangible connection to the past, a reminder of the love and care that went into creating them. As the baby grows older, they may come to appreciate the sentimental value of these items and the stories that accompany them.

In addition to their sentimental value, handmade baby items of knitting also offer practical benefits. The use of natural fibers such as cotton or wool ensures that these items are soft, breathable, and gentle on a baby's delicate skin. Unlike mass-produced items, which may be made from synthetic materials, handmade knitted items are often free from harmful chemicals and dyes, making them a safer choice for babies.

Moreover, the versatility of knitting allows for a wide range of baby items to be created. From cozy blankets and hats to adorable booties and sweaters, the possibilities are endless. Each item can be customized to suit the baby's needs and preferences, making it a truly personalized gift. This level of customization ensures that the item will not only be functional but also aesthetically pleasing, adding an extra layer of joy and satisfaction for the recipient.

The sentimental value and significance of handmade baby items of knitting cannot be overstated. They represent a labor of love, a connection to the past, and a practical yet personalized gift for the baby. These items hold a special place in the hearts of parents and caregivers, serving as a tangible reminder of the care and affection that went into their creation. Whether it's a cozy blanket or a cute hat, these handmade treasures are sure to be cherished for years to come.

Overview of the Book and Navigating Through the Patterns of Knitting:

This book is a comprehensive guide for both beginners and experienced knitters alike. It offers a detailed overview of the art of knitting, providing readers with a solid foundation to explore and create beautiful knitted pieces.

The book begins with an introduction to the history and origins of knitting, tracing its roots back to ancient civilizations and highlighting its evolution over the centuries. This historical context sets the stage for readers to appreciate the rich tradition and craftsmanship associated with knitting.

Next, the book delves into the fundamental techniques of knitting, breaking them down into easy-to-follow steps. From casting on to binding off, readers will learn the essential skills needed to start their knitting journey. The instructions are accompanied by clear illustrations and diagrams, ensuring that even those new to knitting can grasp the concepts with ease.

Once the basics are covered, the book progresses to more advanced techniques and stitches. Readers will learn how to create intricate patterns, cables, lacework, and colorwork, among other techniques. Each technique is explained in detail, with tips and tricks provided to help readers master them. The book also includes a glossary of knitting terms, ensuring that readers can easily understand and follow any knitting pattern they encounter.

One of the standout features of this book is its extensive collection of knitting patterns. From cozy scarves and hats to intricate sweaters and blankets, the book offers a wide range of projects for knitters of all skill levels. Each pattern is accompanied by detailed instructions, including stitch counts, gauge measurements, and yarn recommendations. Additionally, the book provides helpful tips and suggestions for customizing the patterns to suit individual preferences.

To further enhance the learning experience, the book includes a section on troubleshooting common knitting mistakes. From dropped stitches to uneven tension, readers will find solutions to common issues that may arise during their knitting projects. This troubleshooting guide is a valuable resource for both beginners and experienced knitters, helping them overcome obstacles and achieve professional-looking results.

In conclusion, this book is a comprehensive and user-friendly guide that covers all aspects of knitting. From the basics to advanced techniques, the book equips readers with the knowledge and skills needed to create beautiful knitted pieces. With its extensive collection of patterns and troubleshooting guide, this book is a must-have for anyone interested in the art of knitting.

Selecting the Right Yarns for Baby Knits: Materials and Colors: When it comes to knitting baby garments, selecting the right yarns is of utmost importance. Babies have delicate skin that is sensitive to rough textures and harsh materials, so it is crucial to choose yarns that are soft, gentle, and hypoallergenic. Additionally, considering the color of the yarn is also essential as it can affect the overall look and feel of the finished garment.

When it comes to materials, natural fibers are highly recommended for baby knits. Cotton, for instance, is a popular choice due to its softness and breathability. It is gentle on the baby's skin and allows for proper air circulation, preventing overheating and discomfort. Moreover, cotton yarns are easy to care for, making them ideal for busy parents who may not have the time for delicate handwashing.

Another excellent option for baby knits is bamboo yarn. Bamboo is known for its luxurious feel and silky texture, making it incredibly soft against the baby's skin. It is also naturally hypoallergenic and has antibacterial properties, which can help prevent any skin irritations or allergies. Bamboo yarns are also highly absorbent, making them suitable for baby garments that may be prone to spills or accidents.

Merino wool is another popular choice for baby knits, especially for colder climates. Merino wool is incredibly soft and warm, providing excellent insulation for little ones during the winter months. It is also naturally breathable and moisture-wicking, ensuring that the baby stays comfortable and dry. However, it is essential to choose a superwash merino wool, which has been treated to be machine washable, as handwashing delicate baby garments can be time-consuming.

When it comes to colors, pastel shades are often the go-to choice for baby knits. Soft pinks, blues, yellows, and greens create a delicate and soothing aesthetic that is perfect for newborns. These colors are also versatile and can be easily mixed and matched with other baby essentials, such as blankets and accessories. However, it is essential to consider the parents' preferences and the baby's gender, if known, when selecting colors for the knitted garment.

In conclusion, selecting the right yarns for baby knits involves considering both the materials and colors. Natural fibers such as cotton, bamboo, and merino wool are excellent choices due to their softness, breathability, and hypoallergenic properties. Additionally, pastel shades create a soothing and versatile aesthetic for baby garments.

Essential Tools for Knitting Baby Items: When it comes to knitting baby items, having the right tools is essential to ensure that you create high-quality and safe products. Whether you are a beginner or an experienced knitter, there are a few key tools that you should have in your knitting arsenal.

First and foremost, you will need a set of knitting needles. For baby items, it is recommended to use smaller needle sizes, typically ranging from 2.25mm to 4mm. These smaller needles will help you achieve a tighter gauge, resulting in a more durable and comfortable finished product. Circular needles are also a great option for knitting baby items, as they allow you to easily knit in the round and create seamless garments.

Next, you will need a good selection of yarn. When knitting for babies, it is important to choose yarn that is soft, hypoallergenic, and easy to care for. Natural fibers such as cotton, bamboo, and merino wool are popular choices for baby items, as they are gentle on sensitive skin and provide excellent breathability. It is also a good idea to opt for yarn that is machine washable, as baby items tend to get dirty quite often.

In addition to knitting needles and yarn, you will also need a few other tools to help you along the way. A pair of scissors is essential for cutting yarn, so make sure to have a sharp and durable pair on hand. Stitch markers are also useful for keeping track of your stitches, especially when working on more complex patterns. A tape measure or ruler is necessary for checking your gauge and ensuring that your finished item will fit properly. And of course, a yarn needle is needed for weaving in loose ends and finishing off your project.

Lastly, it is always a good idea to have a knitting pattern or two specifically designed for baby items. These patterns will guide you through the process and provide you with the necessary instructions and measurements to create a perfect fit. There are countless baby knitting patterns available online and in knitting books, so you are sure to find something that suits your style and skill level.

In conclusion, knitting baby items requires a specific set of tools to ensure that you create safe and comfortable products. From knitting needles and yarn to scissors and stitch markers, having the right tools will make your knitting experience more enjoyable and your finished items more professional. So gather your essential tools, choose a pattern, and get ready to create beautiful and cozy baby items that will be cherished for years to come.

Creating a Safe and Organized Knitting Space: Creating a safe and organized knitting space is essential for any avid knitter. Not only does it ensure that you can work efficiently and comfortably, but it also helps to prevent accidents and keep your materials in good condition. In this article, we will discuss various tips and strategies to help you create the perfect knitting space.

First and foremost, it is important to choose a suitable location for your knitting area. Ideally, you should select a well-lit and well-ventilated space that is free from distractions. Natural light is particularly beneficial as it allows you to see your stitches more clearly and reduces eye strain. Additionally, good ventilation helps to prevent the accumulation of dust and fibers, which can be detrimental to your health.

Once you have chosen the location, it is time to organize your knitting supplies. Investing in storage solutions such as bins, baskets, or shelves can help keep your yarn, needles, and other accessories neatly organized and easily accessible. Consider categorizing your supplies based on color, weight, or project type to make it easier to find what you need when you need it.

Furthermore, it is crucial to create a safe environment in your knitting space. Ensure that there are no tripping hazards such as loose cables or cluttered pathways. If you have pets or young children, it may be necessary to designate a specific area or use barriers to prevent them from interfering with your knitting. Additionally, be mindful of fire safety by keeping flammable materials away from heat sources and using caution when working with open flames, such as candles or space heaters.

Ergonomics is another important aspect to consider when setting up your knitting space. Investing in a comfortable chair with proper back support and adjustable height can help prevent back and neck strain. Additionally, using a cushion or pillow to support your wrists and elbows can reduce the risk of repetitive strain injuries. It is also advisable to take regular breaks and stretch your muscles to avoid stiffness and discomfort.

In terms of organization, consider creating a system for keeping track of your ongoing projects. This can be as simple as using project bags or folders to store all the necessary materials and patterns together. Labeling your projects with the date started and any relevant notes can also help you stay organized and remember where you left off.

Lastly, don't forget to personalize your knitting space to make it a welcoming and inspiring environment. Hang up artwork or photographs that bring you joy, display finished projects as a source of pride, and incorporate comfortable seating and soft lighting to create a cozy atmosphere.

Basic Knitting Stitches and Techniques: Basic knitting stitches and techniques are essential for anyone interested in learning how to knit. Knitting is a versatile craft that allows you to create beautiful and functional items such as scarves, hats, sweaters, and blankets. Whether you are a beginner or have some experience with knitting, understanding the basic stitches and techniques is crucial for mastering this art form.

One of the most fundamental stitches in knitting is the knit stitch. This stitch creates a smooth and even fabric and is often used as the foundation for many knitting projects. To knit, you insert the right-hand needle into the front of the stitch on the left-hand needle, wrap the yarn around the right-hand needle, and pull it through the stitch, sliding the old stitch off the left-hand needle. This simple motion creates a new stitch on the right-hand needle.

Another important stitch is the purl stitch. The purl stitch creates a bumpy texture and is often used to create ribbing or add variety to a knitting project. To purl, you insert the right-hand needle into the front of the stitch on the left-hand needle, wrap the yarn around the right-hand needle, and pull it through the stitch, sliding the old stitch off the left-hand needle. This motion is similar to the knit stitch but creates a different texture.

Once you have mastered the knit and purl stitches, you can combine them to create various stitch patterns. For example, the stockinette stitch is created by knitting one row and purling the next row. This stitch pattern creates a smooth and flat fabric with one side showing the knit stitches and the other side showing the purl stitches. The garter stitch, on the other hand, is created by knitting every row. This stitch pattern creates a bumpy texture on both sides of the fabric.

In addition to the basic stitches, there are various techniques that can enhance your knitting projects. One such technique is increasing, which allows you to add stitches to your work. Common methods of increasing include knitting or purling into the front and back of a stitch, or using yarn overs to create new stitches. Decreasing, on the other hand, involves removing stitches from your work. Common methods of decreasing include knitting or purling two stitches together, or slipping a stitch and passing it over another stitch.

Reading and Understanding Knitting Patterns: Reading and understanding knitting patterns is an essential skill for any knitter, whether you are a beginner or an experienced crafter. Knitting patterns provide the instructions and guidance needed to create a specific project, such as a sweater, hat, or scarf. However, they can sometimes be overwhelming and confusing, especially for those who are new to knitting.

To effectively read and understand knitting patterns, it is important to familiarize yourself with the various components and abbreviations commonly used in these patterns. The first step is to carefully read through the entire pattern before starting your project. This will give you an overview of the required materials, gauge, and any special techniques or stitches that may be involved.

One of the most important aspects of a knitting pattern is the gauge. Gauge refers to the number of stitches and rows per inch that you need to achieve in order for your finished project to match the size specified in the pattern. It is crucial to check your gauge before starting your project, as using the wrong needle size or yarn weight can result in a significantly different finished product.

Another key element of knitting patterns is the abbreviations. Knitting patterns often use abbreviations to save space and make the instructions more concise. Common abbreviations include "k" for knit, "p" for purl, "yo" for yarn over, and "ssk" for slip, slip, knit. It is important to familiarize yourself with these abbreviations and their corresponding stitches to ensure that you can follow the pattern accurately.

In addition to abbreviations, knitting patterns may also include special techniques or stitches that are specific to the project. These can include cables, lacework, colorwork, or shaping techniques. If you are unfamiliar with any of these techniques, it is helpful to refer to knitting resources, such as books or online tutorials, to learn and practice them before attempting the pattern.

When reading a knitting pattern, it is also important to pay attention to the specific instructions for each section of the project. This includes the cast-on method, the stitch pattern, any shaping or increases/decreases, and the finishing techniques. Take your time to carefully read and understand each step before proceeding, as mistakes can be difficult to correct once you have progressed further in the project.

If you find yourself struggling to understand a knitting pattern, don't hesitate to seek help from more experienced knitters or join a knitting group or class. These resources can provide guidance and support, as well as offer tips and tricks for successfully completing your"

Tips for Knitting for Babies: Safety and Comfort: When it comes to knitting for babies, safety and comfort should be the top priorities. Babies have delicate skin and are more susceptible to allergies and irritations, so it is crucial to choose the right materials and follow certain guidelines to ensure their well-being.

First and foremost, selecting the right yarn is essential. Opt for soft, hypoallergenic yarns that are gentle on the baby's skin. Natural fibers like cotton, bamboo, and merino wool are great choices as they are breathable and less likely to cause irritation. Avoid using synthetic yarns that may contain harmful chemicals or irritants.

Additionally, consider the size of the yarn and needles. Thinner yarns and smaller needles are ideal for baby knits as they create a softer and more comfortable fabric. Avoid using bulky or textured yarns that may be uncomfortable for the baby.

When it comes to patterns, choose designs that prioritize safety. Avoid using buttons, beads, or any small embellishments that can pose a choking hazard. Instead, opt for seamless patterns or those with minimal embellishments. If you do choose to add buttons or other fasteners, ensure they are securely attached and cannot be easily pulled off.

Another important aspect to consider is the fit of the knitted items. Babies grow quickly, so it is crucial to knit with room for growth. Avoid tight-fitting garments that may restrict movement or cause discomfort. Opt for patterns with adjustable features like buttoned or tie closures that can accommodate different sizes.

In terms of care, it is important to wash all knitted items before use to remove any potential irritants or chemicals. Use a gentle, baby-safe detergent and avoid using fabric softeners or harsh chemicals that can irritate the baby's skin. Always follow the care instructions provided with the yarn to ensure the longevity and quality of the knitted items.

Lastly, always supervise babies when they are wearing knitted items. While knitting for babies is a wonderful way to show love and care, it is important to remember that babies can be unpredictable and may pull or tug at their clothing. Regularly check the knitted items for any signs of wear or loose threads that may pose a safety risk.

In conclusion, knitting for babies requires careful consideration of safety and comfort. By choosing the right materials, patterns, and fit, and following proper care instructions, you can create beautiful and safe knitted items that will keep babies cozy and comfortable.

Basic Baby Sweater: Step-by-Step Guide of Knitting: The basic baby sweater is a classic knitting project that is perfect for beginners or anyone looking for a quick and satisfying project. In this step-by-step guide, we will walk you through the process of knitting a basic baby sweater, from choosing the right yarn and needles to finishing touches.

1. Gather your materials: To start knitting a basic baby sweater, you will need a few essential materials. First, choose a soft and comfortable yarn suitable for babies, such as a baby or sport weight yarn. You will also need a pair of knitting needles in the appropriate size for your chosen yarn. Additionally, you may want to have stitch markers, a tapestry needle, and buttons or other closures for the sweater.

2. Choose a pattern: There are countless patterns available for knitting baby sweaters, ranging from simple to more intricate designs. For beginners, it is recommended to start with a basic pattern that uses simple stitches and techniques. Look for patterns that provide clear instructions and include a size chart to ensure a proper fit for the baby.

3. Gauge swatch: Before diving into the sweater, it is important to knit a gauge swatch to determine the correct tension for your project. Follow the instructions provided in the pattern to knit a small square using the recommended needle size. Measure the number of stitches and rows per inch and compare it to the gauge specified in the pattern. Adjust your needle size if necessary to achieve the correct gauge.

4. Cast on: Once you have determined the correct gauge, it's time to cast on the required number of stitches for the size you are making. The pattern will specify the cast-on method to use, such as the long-tail cast-on or the knitted cast-on. Take your time and make sure your stitches are even and not too tight.

5. Knit the body: The body of the baby sweater is usually worked in one piece from the bottom up. Follow the pattern instructions for the stitch pattern and shaping. Common stitches used for the body include stockinette stitch, garter stitch, or a combination of both. Pay attention to any increases or decreases specified in the pattern to shape the sweater.

6. Knit the sleeves: After completing the body, it's time to knit the sleeves. Depending on the pattern, you may knit them separately and then sew them onto the body, or you may pick up stitches along the armholes and knit them in the round. Follow the pattern instructions for the sleeve length and shaping.

Playful Patterns and Colors of Knitting: This book is a vibrant and visually appealing collection of knitted items that showcase a wide range of playful patterns and colors. This output is the result of the creative process of knitting, where various techniques and stitches are used to create intricate and eye-catching designs.

When it comes to patterns, the output of this book offers an extensive variety. From classic and timeless patterns like stripes and polka dots to more intricate and complex designs like cables and lace, there is something for everyone. These patterns are carefully chosen and thoughtfully incorporated into the knitted items to create a visually stunning effect.

In addition to patterns, the output of this book also focuses on the use of colors. Knitting allows for endless possibilities when it comes to color combinations, and this collection takes full advantage of that. Bold and vibrant colors are often used to create a striking contrast, while softer and more muted tones are used to create a subtle and elegant look. The use of color in knitting adds depth and dimension to the finished items, making them truly unique and eye-catching.

The output of this book is not just limited to a specific type of item. It encompasses a wide range of knitted items, including but not limited to sweaters, scarves, hats, socks, and blankets. Each item is carefully crafted with attention to detail, ensuring that the patterns and colors are seamlessly integrated into the design.

Furthermore, the output of this book is not just limited to traditional knitting techniques. It also explores and incorporates modern and innovative techniques, such as colorwork and intarsia, to create even more intricate and captivating designs. These techniques allow for the creation of complex patterns and color combinations that were once thought to be impossible in knitting.

Overall, the output of this book is a celebration of creativity and self-expression through the art of knitting. It showcases the endless possibilities that knitting offers in terms of patterns and colors, and it serves as an inspiration for both experienced knitters and beginners alike. Whether you are looking for a bold and vibrant statement piece or a subtle and elegant accessory, this collection has something to offer for everyone who appreciates the beauty of playful patterns and colors in knitting.

Washing and Maintaining Baby Knits: Washing and maintaining baby knits is an essential part of caring for your little one's clothing. Baby knits are delicate and require special attention to ensure they stay soft, comfortable, and in good condition. In this guide, we will provide you with detailed instructions on how to properly wash and maintain baby knits, so you can keep them looking and feeling their best.

First and foremost, it is important to read the care instructions on the label of the baby knit garment. These instructions will provide you with specific guidelines on how to wash and care for the item. Follow these instructions carefully to avoid any damage to the fabric or shrinking.

When it comes to washing baby knits, it is best to hand wash them. Fill a basin or sink with lukewarm water and add a mild detergent specifically designed for baby clothes. Gently agitate the water to create suds. Place the baby knit garment in the water and gently swish it around, making sure to fully immerse it. Avoid rubbing or scrubbing the fabric, as this can cause stretching or pilling.

After a few minutes of soaking, drain the soapy water and refill the basin with clean lukewarm water. Rinse the baby knit garment thoroughly, ensuring all the detergent is removed. Repeat this rinsing process if necessary.

Once the garment is rinsed, gently squeeze out the excess water. Avoid wringing or twisting the fabric, as this can cause it to lose its shape. Lay a clean towel flat on a surface and place the baby knit garment on top. Roll the towel up, with the garment inside, and gently press down to absorb more water. Repeat this process with a dry towel if needed.

After removing excess water, reshape the baby knit garment to its original form. Lay it flat on a clean, dry towel or a drying rack. Avoid hanging the garment to dry, as this can cause it to stretch or lose its shape. Allow the garment to air dry completely before storing or using it again.

In terms of maintaining baby knits, it is important to handle them with care. Avoid exposing them to rough surfaces or sharp objects that can snag or tear the fabric. Keep them away from Velcro or other fasteners that can cause pilling or damage.

To prevent excessive wear and tear, it is recommended to rotate your baby's knitted garments. This means not using the same item every day, but rather alternating between different pieces.

Advanced Baby Knit Projects: Advanced Baby Knit Projects is a comprehensive guide that caters to experienced knitters who are looking to take their skills to the next level by creating intricate and beautiful projects for babies. This book is designed to provide a wide range of patterns and techniques that will challenge and inspire knitters to create unique and stunning pieces for the little ones in their lives.

The book begins with an introduction that highlights the benefits of knitting for babies, such as the ability to create personalized and handmade items that are not only practical but also sentimental. It also emphasizes the importance of choosing the right materials and tools for advanced projects, as well as providing tips on how to read and interpret complex knitting patterns.

The subsequent chapters delve into various advanced knitting techniques, such as lace knitting, cable knitting, and colorwork. Each technique is explained in detail, with step-by-step instructions and accompanying photographs to ensure that knitters can easily follow along and master the techniques. The book also includes helpful tips and tricks for troubleshooting common issues that may arise during the knitting process.

The heart of Advanced Baby Knit Projects lies in its extensive collection of patterns. From delicate lace bonnets to cozy cable-knit blankets, the book offers a wide range of projects that showcase the versatility and creativity of advanced knitting. Each pattern is accompanied by detailed instructions, including stitch counts, gauge measurements, and suggested yarns, ensuring that knitters have all the information they need to successfully complete each project.

In addition to the patterns, the book also features inspirational photographs of the finished projects, showcasing the beauty and intricacy of each design. These photographs serve as a visual guide and source of inspiration for knitters, allowing them to envision the final product and customize it to their own preferences.

Advanced Baby Knit Projects also includes a section on customization and personalization, encouraging knitters to add their own unique touches to the patterns. Whether it's incorporating different colors, adding embellishments, or modifying the sizing, this section provides guidance and ideas for making each project truly one-of-a-kind.

Overall, Advanced Baby Knit Projects is a must-have resource for experienced knitters who are looking to expand their skills and create stunning projects for babies. With its detailed instructions, comprehensive patterns, and inspirational photographs, this book is sure to inspire and delight knitters of all levels.

CHAPTER 1: CHOOSING YOUR MATERIALS

A baby's skin is sensitive so the first consideration when choosing the yarn for your baby project is the softness. You'll find many yarns designated as "baby yarn". This has nothing to do with the content, weight, or gauge, but simply that the yarn is both soft and easy care, so it is ideal for anything intended to be worn or wrapped around an infant.

Knitting yarns for baby projects can range from fingering to bulky, depending on how delicate or chunky you want your finished product to be. An heirloom quality, christening gown, for example, might be knit in a fingering weight cotton, which shows off intricate details.

You will also find some fluffier yarns in bulky or super bulky weights. These yarns are perfect for blankets and sweaters. Another benefit of bulky and super bulky yarn is it is very thick and knits up quickly.

YARN STANDARDS

The Craft Yarn Council set the standards for categories, gauges, and recommended needle sizes, so you'll see one of these symbols on the yarn's label:

YARN WEIGHT	(0) LACE	(1) SUPER FINE	(2) FINE	(3) LIGHT	(4) MEDIUM	(5) BULKY	(6) SUPER BULKY
YARN TYPE	10-count crochet thread, Fingering	Baby, Fingering, Sock	Baby, Sport	Dk, Light Worsted	Afghan, Aran, Worsted	Chunky, Craft, Rug	Bulky, Roving
METRIC NEEDLE SIZE (mm)	1.5-2.25	2.25-3.25	3.25-3.75	3.75-4.5	4.5-5.5	5.5-8	8 or larger
US NEEDLE SIZE	000-1	1-3	3-5	5-7	7-9	9-11	11 or larger
UK / CDN NEEDLE SIZE	17-13	13-10	10-9	9-7	7-5	5-0	0 or larger
JPN NEEDLE SIZE	0	0-3	3-5	5-8	8-11	11-8mm	8mm or larger
4" GAUGE IN STOCKINETTE STITCH	33-40 sts	27-32 sts	23-26 sts	21-24 sts	16-20 sts	12-15 sts	6-11 sts

Whenever you are considering a pattern, be sure to note the suggested yarn category. Sure, there are plenty of seasoned knitters who fall in love with a particular yarn, buy it, and then go looking for a pattern that will work with the fiber and the gauge. I do not recommend this for a beginner.

You'll end up either (a) spending a lot of time recalculating an entire pattern and working numerous swatches to match the gauge; or (b) growing a large stash of yarn that may or may not ever find its way into a knitted garment. I am guilty of this second count, as my numerous bins of yarn demonstrate.

You should take note of the yarn weight category specified in the pattern (e.g., Fingering, Worsted) so you do not have to turn your pattern into a math test. If your pattern calls for a worsted weight yarn, aim for worsted, and the most you'll have to do is change your needle size to adjust to the gauge.

FIBER FIRST

Another important consideration is the yarn's fiber. You should choose a soft fiber as well as something that will be easy to care for. Babies make messes—at both ends—so make sure whatever you knit is machine washable. Otherwise, it will probably be tucked away in a drawer.

Just as you probably buy silk or linen clothing for an infant, you should pay attention to the care directions for the yarn you are going to use. Natural fibers like cotton and bamboo are great because they stand up to machine washing. However, even purists who generally knit only with natural fibers concede that a little acrylic is acceptable for this type of knitting. Many fibers are blended with acrylic for easy care, so you can get the best of both worlds this way. I used to be a fiber diva and turned up my nose at acrylic—because it pilled terribly—but yarn manufacturers have come a long way toward creating manmade fibers that look and feel great.

For warmth with softness, you do not have to cross "wool" off your list of acceptable fibers for baby knits. "Superwool" or "Washable Wool" is a wool fiber that has been treated to avoid the fiber's natural inclination to shrink when tossed in the washer or dryer. The core is wool so it still has the soft loftiness of this beautiful fiber, but can go through the wash cycle without coming out five sizes smaller.

NEEDLE KNOW-HOW

Next, you choose your needles. The size will be dictated by the yarn's weight and pattern gauge, but the type of needle is up to you. This chart provides you with a quick guide.

STANDARD NEEDLE AND YARN SIZES

WEIGHT	NEEDLE (US)	GAUGE (st/4 in)
0 (Lace)	000 – 1	33 - 40 sts
1 (Fingering, Sock)	1 - 3	27 - 32 sts
2 (Sport, Baby)	3 - 5	23 - 26 sts
3 (DK, Light Worsted)	5 - 7	21 - 24
4 (Worsted, Aran)	7 - 9	16 - 20
5 (Bulky, Chunky)	9 - 11	12 - 15
6 (Super Bulky)	11 +	6 - 11

Needles can be made of plastic, aluminum, nickel-plated, wood (walnut, rosewood, cherry, birch), and bamboo (it is a plant, not wood). Let me just say that no one should knit with plastic needles. Sure, they bend (which also means they break) and come in fun colors, but the yarn does not glide as well. And who needs more plastic in their life?

I also suggest bypassing aluminum needles, for the total opposite reasons of why I discourage using plastic needles. Aluminum is slippery, so stitches can easily fall off your needle. Plus, the metal is so rigid that it is hard on your hands and fingers.

Wood, bamboo, or nickel-plated are the best options for knitting needles. I personally prefer bamboo or wood. The nickel-plated needles are wonderful and experienced knitters enjoy the faster speed they can get, but I just love putting two fibers—yarn and wood—together.

KNITTING NEEDLES COME IN THREE BASIC TYPES

-Straight: The classic knitting needle—straight, with one pointed end and one blunt end. Straight needles come in a variety of lengths, usually from nine to 14 inches in length.

-Circular: Two short needles are joined together with a thin, flexible cable, which varies in length.

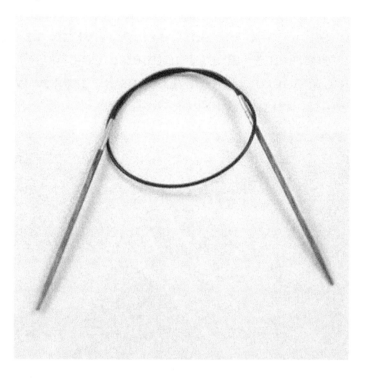

-Double-pointed: These needles have points on each end. They are designed for knitting a small circumference (socks, cuffs, necklines) in the round, seamlessly. You work end to end, without turning the work, and slide your stitches from one end to the next. When working in stockinette in the round, you knit every round (unless instructed otherwise) because you are NOT working back and forth. This is a bonus for people who aren't fans of (1) turning their work, and (2) stitching up seams.

Knitting newbies are often fearful of double-pointed needles. My advice? Get over it! It does not take long to master these little gems, and you'll be glad you did, particularly if you ever want to make hats, booties, mittens, and sweaters.

When you buy a set of double-pointed needles, you'll probably get five needles in the package. Americans, for whatever reason, tend to only work with four. You spread your stitches across three of them and then knit with the fourth one. Europeans tend to space out their stitches across four needles and knit with the fifth. Unless you have a large piece with lots of stitches, the four-needle method is great—and you have one less needle to deal with.

OTHER TOOLS FOR YOUR KNITTING BAG

One of the wonderful things about knitting is that you do not need a bunch of tools. You can buy them, sure, but they are not essential. When you are working on a small project, like baby clothes, it is very portable. All you need is the knitting, the pattern, and a couple of gotta-haves, which I keep in a small cosmetic bag.

-Row Counter: With some patterns, you will follow a specific combination of stitches that change from row to row (like the Lacy Blanket found later in this guide). In this instance, it is helpful to have a tool to keep track of where you are in the pattern. You can write the row numbers on a Post-it note or index card and cross them off as you complete them. You can also mark the pattern as you go, or buy a row counter and click off the row numbers—just make sure no one else gets hold of this gadget and changes your row!

-Stitch Gauge: This handy dandy tool is a small piece of metal or plastic with a tiny window, a ruler and a bunch of holes in graduated sizes. You line up your stitches in the little window so you can measure the number of stitches per inch on a swatch. The holes correspond to needle sizes. If your needle does not have the size marked on it (which often happens with double-pointed needles), slip it through these holes to find the one that fits as perfectly as Cinderella's slipper.

-Stitch Markers: In some cases, you need to leave a marker, usually when working a pattern stitch or knitting in the round. They are small rings that you slip on your needle. You move them from needle to needle as you continue working. In this book, you'll use markers on the Baby Blossom Hat, Little Fisherman's Hat, and Lacy Blanket (All found later in this guide) to keep track of where you work the pattern stitch.

-Stitch Holder*:* When you need to set aside the stitches to be worked, a stitch holder is the perfect tool. A stitch holder looks like an oversized safety pin and comes in various sizes—small ones for a few stitches and larger ones for big jobs (e.g., necks). You'll use stitch holders for the Color Blocked Cardigan (Found later in this guide).

-Point Protectors: These little rubber knobs stick on the ends of your needle, preventing your work from slipping off. This is especially helpful when you have many stitches on a needle, like the double-pointed variety. You can also cut a wine cork in half, but that means you have to open a bottle. Oh, well…

-Darning Needle: Looking like a really large sewing needle, a darning needle features a blunt tip (i.e., you will not prick your finger with it). They are handy for weaving in the tail end of a piece of yarn at the start or finish of the mitten or thumb, or where you've joined two skeins together.

-Measuring Tape: If you want to get the fit just right, you need to measure your work!

CHAPTER 2: KNITTING BASICS

Knitting for a baby is a labor of love. You are creating a one-of-a-kind item for a one-of-a-kind infant. From choosing the pattern, yarn, and colors to customizing the project to the size of the baby, it is personal from start to finish.

Your best bet for knitting something that fits the baby, is to get measurements. If it is not your child you are knitting for, you can ask what size the child is wearing. You can also ask to measure an item of clothing that fits the baby (if you are knitting something for later, be sure to adjust the measurements).

HERE ARE SOME STANDARD MEASUREMENTS FOR YOUR REFERENCE:

Measurement	3 months	6 months	12 months	18 months	24 months
Chest	16"/40.5cm	17"/43cm	18"/45.5cm	19"/48cm	20"/50.5cm
Center Back, Neck to Cuff	10.5"/26.5cm	11.5"/29cm	12.5"/31.5cm	14"/35.5cm	18"/45.5cm
Back Waist Length	6"/15.5cm	7"/17.5cm	7.5"/19cm	8"/20.5cm	8.5"/21.5cm
Shoulder to Shoulder	7.25"/18.5cm	7.75"/19.5cm	8.25"/21cm	8.5"/21.5cm	8.75"/22cm
Underarm to Wrist	6"/15.5cm	6.5"/16.5cm	7.5"/19cm	8"/20.5cm	8.5"/21.5cm
Armhole Depth	3.25"/8.5cm	3.5"/9cm	3.75"/9.5cm	4"/10cm	4.25"/10.5cm
Waist	18"/45.5cm	19"/48cm	20"/50.5cm	20.5"/52cm	21"/53.5cm
Hips	19"/48cm	20"/50.5cm	20"/50.5cm	21"/53.5cm	22"/56cm

GAUGE YOUR KNITTING

Do you knit tightly or loosely? Is the yarn you've chosen different from the one specified in the pattern?

The best way to ensure the piece you are knitting will size up with the pattern you've chosen is to knit a sample swatch. There are many factors that contribute to the gauge of your knitting, so it just makes sense to knit up a small swatch (4" x 4") to double-check. Every pattern will provide a gauge; this number shows how the stitch count of the pattern was calculated, given in stitches and rows per inch.

Sadly, this step is often ignored by knitters. I admit, in my over-confident youth, I rarely knitted a sample swatch, but after several times of ending up with a sizeable piece I had to unravel, I learned to take 10 minutes at the start knit a swatch. It is a safety precaution that requires such little effort that you will thank yourself for later.

Start by looking at your pattern. What's the gauge? Compare this measurement to the one on the yarn label. Try to choose a yarn that has the same gauge as your pattern (or darn close). You can make adjustments to the swatch by changing the needle size—bigger or smaller—but you need to understand that using a larger needle than recommended will create a loose-knit that might look like it has holes. On the opposite end of this spectrum, using a smaller needle size produces a denser, tighter fabric with less drape.

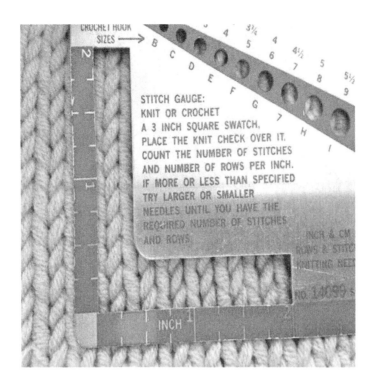

The best way to make sure you get the right width is to knit a swatch. I like to use 20 stitches for my swatches, because it breaks down into easy multiples. For example: half = 10 stitches; quarter = 5 stitches. That way, when I measure the width of the finished sample, it is easier to more accurately calculate how many stitches I have per inch. You need to know how many stitches per inch, so that you can multiply that number by the number of inches in circumference that you want.

For example, you knit a sample using 20 stitches. The width of your finished sample is 4 inches. That means that with this yarn on these needles, you are knitting 5 stitches per inch. If you want a hat, for example, that measures 8 inches around, you would need to work 40 stitches (8 inches X 5 stitches/inch).

CASTING ON

The first step to knitting is called "casting on". There are many methods of casting on. Some types are more suitable for particular projects, but the long-tail cast-on is universal. You'll never go wrong by mastering this method!

Start by measuring a length of yarn. With Worsted weight yarn, allow 1 inch for each stitch you will be casting on. If you are using a Bulky or Chunky yarn and big needles, you'll need 1.5 to 2 inches per stitch. If you are using finer yarn and smaller needles, you'll need about a half-inch of yarn per casted stitch. For any of these, I usually add about 6 inches to my total, just to be safe.

Don't cut the yarn. Just hold it where you've measured your desired length.

-Step One: Make a slip knot at the point where you've marked the length of your yarn for casting on. Slip the loop over one needle and pull the tail to tighten it.

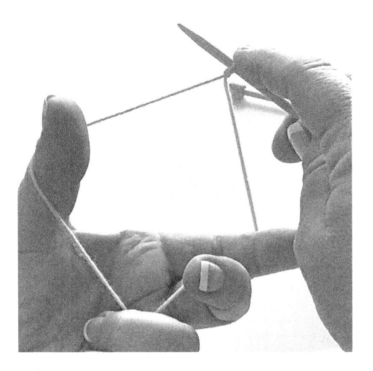

-Step Two: Hold the needle in your right hand with your index finger on top, holding the slip knot in place.

-Step Three: With your left hand under the needle, wrap one strand around your index finger and the other around your thumb. You should have a triangle shape with your needle at the top point and your two fingers making the two points for the triangle base.

-Step Four: Bring the needle down so the yarn makes a "V" between your thumb and forefinger, which are now positioned like your pointing a gun.

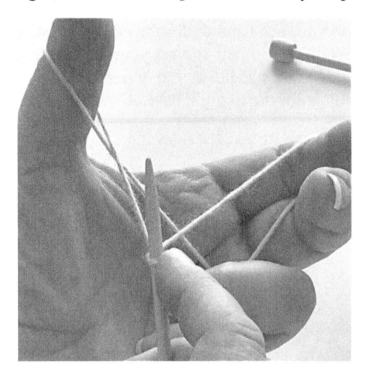

-Step Five: With your right hand, guide the point of the needle under the left side of the yarn that is looped around your thumb.

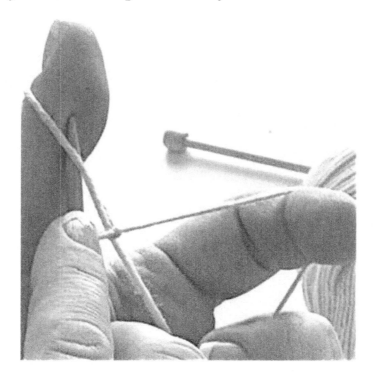

-Step Six: Guide the needle UNDER this point and OVER the yarn on the right side of your thumb.

-Step Seven: Move the tip of the needle OVER the left side of the yarn on your index finger.

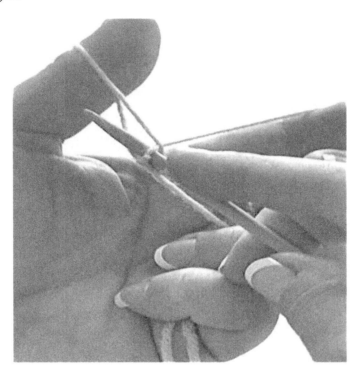

-Step Eight: Swing the needle back to the left, THROUGH the loop on your thumb, entering it from the right side of the loop and coming through the left side of it.

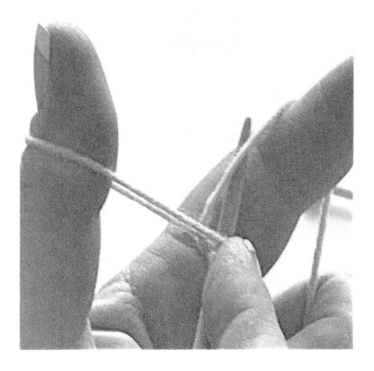

-Step Nine: You will see that you have a loop on your needle now. Pull your needle up and release the yarn on your finger. Then pull the two yarn ends to tighten the casted on stitch.

The cast-on follows this pattern: under your thumb, over your index finger, and back through the thumb loop. Use this as your Cast-on Mantra: Under-Over-Through, Under-Over-Through...

Congratulations! You have your first stitch. Personally, I think casting on is the most complicated part of knitting. Once you master this, the rest will be easy.

THE KNIT STITCH

To begin, hold the needle with the cast-on stitches in your left hand, with your hand on top of the needle. Your index finger should rest on top of the stitches, holding them in place.

There are two strands of yarn hanging down. The tail is the yarn left over from your cast-on. The other is what we call the "working strand", which is attached to your skein of yarn. Beginning knitters often make the mistake of knitting with the tail. Then they get partway through the row and run out of yarn. Then have to "un-knit" the stitches all the way back to the beginning of the row—which isn't fun.

To avoid this "uh-oh" moment, I always tuck the long tail under my fingers and away from the working strand.

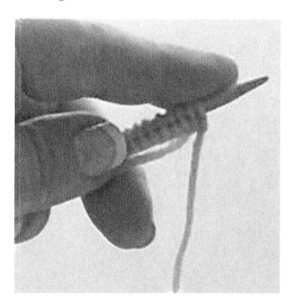

-Step One: Holding your empty needle in your right hand, insert the tip under the front of the first cast-on stitch. Push the needle through the loop and behind the needle with the stitches, forming a criss-cross with the two needles.

-Step Two: Hold the criss-crossed needles together with the thumb and forefinger of your left hand.

-Step Three: With your right hand, wrap the working strand COUNTER-CLOCKWISE around the needle in the back. Pull it forward, between the criss-crossed needles.

-Step Four: Slowly slide the back needle down until the loop is almost at the end of the tip (about a half-inch to an inch from the point).

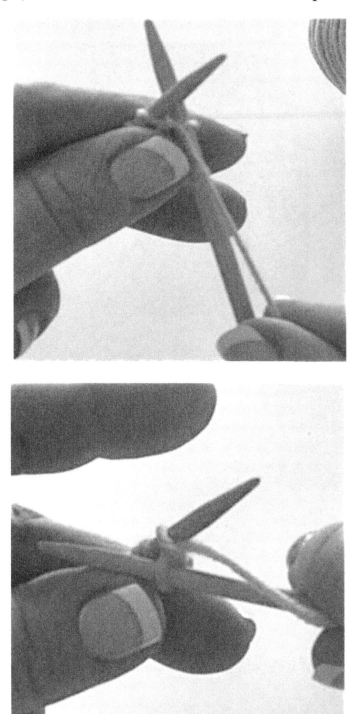

-Step Five: With your right hand holding the working needle and the working strand in place, point the tip of the needle downward and into the front of the loop on the left needle. This is the same front loop that you started with.

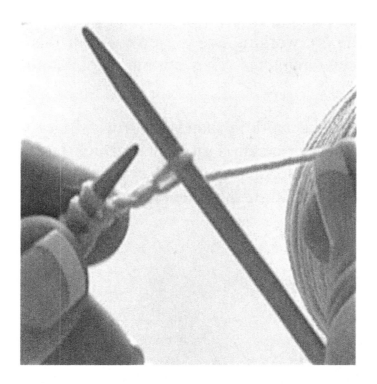

What you've done here is gone into that first loop, wrapped the yarn around the working needle to create a loop, and then brought it back through where you started.

-Step Six: Pull your right needle up and slide the stitch off the left needle, keeping the loop on your right needle. This is your first knit stitch!

GET INTO YOUR RHYTHM

Just like casting on, the knit stitch feels awkward at first. With practice, you'll develop the muscle memory that makes it mindless. If you've ever seen those knitters chatting or watching something other than their knitting while their fingers are working away, they can knit this way because the motion is completely ingrained. They are running on auto-knitter. And you will, too—eventually.

In circular knitting, you work in rounds, not rows. Since you are not going back and forth, you can create a stockinette stitch just by knitting every round. If you want a knitted garment that has reverse stockinette, you'll purl every round instead of knitting the stitches.

AVOID THE LADDER EFFECT

When working on double-pointed needles, knitters can experience a situation known as "the ladder effect". This happens when the stitches on the end of each needle have too much slack. As you keep knitting in the round, you'll see a column of loose stitches that resembles a ladder.

To avoid this unsightly problem, as soon as you move from one double-pointed needle to the next, pull the working strand tightly. This will close up any gaps that could lead to ladder rungs in your finished piece.

THE PURL STITCH

A purl stitch is the opposite of a knit stitch. With the knit stitch, the needle points behind the needle that holds the stitches from the previous row. The purl stitch is worked to the front of that needle. Instead of sliding your working needle up and under the stitch you are going to knit, you come in from the top and go down.

Let's break it down.

-Step One: Holding your empty needle in your right hand, insert the tip under the front of the first stitch, coming at it from the top, so the working needle is pointing downward. Form a criss-cross with the two needles. Your working needle should be on top of the one that is holding the stitches.

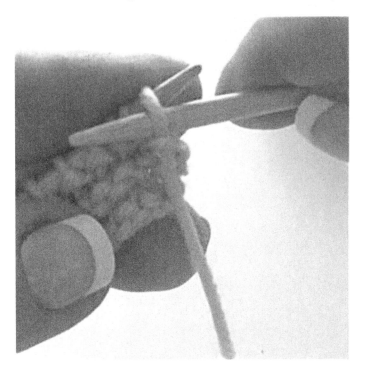

-Step Two: Hold the criss-crossed needles together with the thumb and forefinger of your left hand.

-Step Three: With your right hand, wrap the working strand COUNTER-CLOCKWISE around the needle in the front.

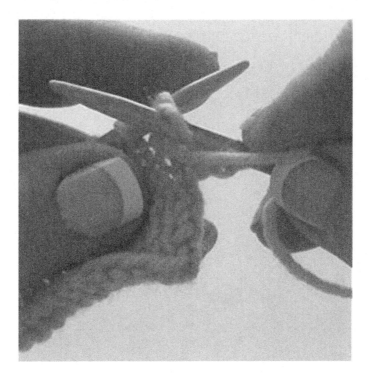

-Step Four: Slowly slide the forward needle backward until the loop is almost at the end of the tip (about a half-inch to an inch from the point).

-Step Five: With your right hand holding the working needle and the working strand in place, point the tip of the needle backward and up into the front of the loop on the left needle. Your working needle should now be behind the left needle and inside the loop.

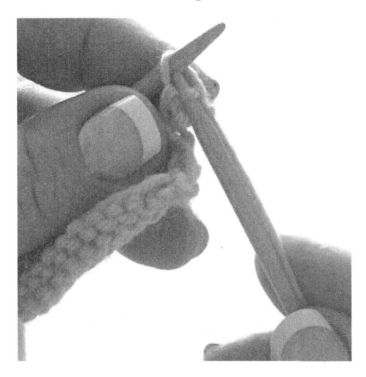

-Step Six: Pull your right needle up and slide the stitch off the left needle, keeping the loop on your right needle.

STOCKINETTE STITCH

Stockinette is what most people consider knitting. It has a flat front and a ridged back. The stitch is created by alternately knitting a row of knit stitches and a row of purl stitches. The result is a knitted fabric that has a pattern of "V's" on one side and ridges on the other.

Some patterns might call for a "reverse stockinette". This simply means that the purl side (the bumpy one) is considered the right side of the fabric.

RIBBED STITCH

Once you get comfortable working in rows of knit and rows of purl, you can take your knitting skill to the next step—creating a rib.

Ribbing has an elastic quality. It is used on cuffs, neckbands, and waistbands to provide some "give" to the garment.

Ribbing requires that you knit and purl within the same row. For example, a 2-2 Rib is done by working 2 knit stitches and then 2 purl stitches. You repeat the pattern across the row.

CAUTION: When you are working knit and purl in the same row, **be very careful** to move your working strand forward and back to correspond with the stitch. For example, if you've just purled, then your strand will be in front of your working needle. Before knitting the next stitch, flip the working strand back between the two needles, so it is behind them. If you do not remember to move your working strand, you will end up with gaping holes! I suggest you practice ribbing by making a swatch before you dive into knitting a project. Get the rhythm of moving your working strand back and forth.

CHAPTER 3: CHECKERBOARD BABY WASHCLOTH

A cotton washcloth is a great project for a beginner—or anyone. Pick the stitch pattern you like and you can create a great variety of washcloths, in an array of colors.

Materials:

-100 yards of Worsted weight cotton yarn (#4)

-Size 6 needles

Gauge:

-4 stitches: 1 inch

Finished Size:

-9" X 9"

Abbreviations:

-*Pm*: Place stitch marker.

Instructions:

-Cast on 45 stitches.

-Knit 6 rows.

Pattern Stitch:

-Row 1: K5, pm, *K5, P5*; repeat across row to last 5 sts, pm; K5

-Row 2: K5, pm, *P5, K5*; repeat across row to last 5 sts, pm; K5

-Rows 3 and 5: Repeat Row 1.

-Rows 4 and 6: Repeat Row 2.

-Row 7: K5, pm, *P5, K5*; repeat across row to last 5 sts, pm; K5

-Row 8: K5, pm, *K5, P5*; repeat across row to last 5 sts, pm; K5

-Rows 9 and 11: Repeat Row 7.

-Rows 10 and 12: Repeat Row 8.

-Repeat Rows 1 through 12 four more times.

-Knit 6 rows.

-Bind off.

CHAPTER 4: BEGINNER BABY SOCKS

Sock knitting is addictive, and when you are making up to tiny ones, they work up quickly. This means that you can easily give your special baby a wide variety of cozy socks to keep their teeny, tiny toes warm.

Materials:

-110 yards of Fingering/Sock weight yarn (#1)

-Size 2 double-pointed needles

Gauge:

-7 stitches = 1 inch

Finished Size:

-Foot measures 3" (heel to toe) for Small (newborn); 3.5" for Medium; 4" for Large. Instructions given are for Small, with changes for Medium and Large in parentheses.

Abbreviations:

-K2tog: Slip the working needle under the next 2 stitches on the left needles and knit them together. This creates a right-slanting decrease.

-SSK: Slip the next stitch from the left needle to the right as if you're going to knit, without working it; slip the second stitch in the same way (do these one at a time, not together). Then knit them together by slipping the left needle into the FRONT of the two stitches. This creates a left-slanting decrease.

-Sl1 pwise: Slip the first stitch as if you are going to purl.

-Pm: Place stitch marker.

Instructions:

Leg:

-Cast on 20 (24, 28) stitches. Work ribbing as knit 1, purl 1 (K1, P1) for 2 inches (or desired length of cuff.

Heel Flap:

-Knit 1 round evenly.

-Row 1: For the flap, you will work half of your total stitches: 10 (12, 14). Slip first stitch as if to knit 9 (11, 13) stitches and turn work.

-Row 2: Slip first stitch as if to purl, and then purl across 9 (11, 13) stitches and turn work.

-Repeats Rows 1 and 2—8 (10, 12) times.

Turn the Heel:

Once you have the back of the heel done, you need to create a 90-degree turn on the bottom in order to start the foot. Starting from the bottom of the heel flap, you'll continue to work back and forth, from the center of the heel, and then pick up one stitch at the end of reach row to build the bottom of the heel.

Here's how the heel turn is worked:

-Row 1: (Right side) Knit to the center of the heel (half the stitches on your heel): 5 (6, 7), SSK, K1. Turn your work so the purl side is facing you (leave the remaining stitches that you have not worked, because you'll work one stitch, one row at a time).

-Row 2: (Wrong side) Sl1, P1, P2tog, P1.

-Row 3: Sl1, K2, SSK, K1.

-Row 4: Sl1 pwise, P3, P2tog, P1—6 sts remain.

For Medium Only:

-Row 5: Sl1, K4, SSK.

-Row 6: Sl1 pwise, P5, P2tog—6 sts remain.

For Large Only:

-Row 5: Sl1, K4, SSK, K1.

-Row 6: Sl1 pwise, P5, P2tog, P1—8 sts remain.

SHAPE THE GUSSET

The gusset is the triangular part of the sock between the heel and the foot. This is where you start "re-growing" your stitches to set up for knitting the foot of the sock. If you can pick up stitches, you can shape a gusset.

Remember how you slipped the first stitch of each row on the heel flap? Well, that created a nice pattern of stitches to be picked up, as shown in the next photo.

-Start the shaping by knitting across the 6 (6, 8) remaining heel stitches. Then pick up the stitches along the edge of the heel (we are calling this "Needle 1"). If you worked 10 (12, 14) rows of the heel flap pattern, you should have a total of 5 (6, 7) stitches to pick up.

-Knit in pattern across the instep (the top of the foot) (this is "Needle 2").

-Using another needle, pick up and knit stitches along the other side of the heel (Needle 3). Divide the total *heel* stitches—16 (18, 22) evenly between Needles 1 and 3.

-You're going to return to working in the round again now. Your goal now for the gusset is to decrease the stitches until you have the same number of stitches on your heel as the instep—10 (12, 14).

Here's how you work the decreases:

-Round 1: Knit across Needle 1 to last 2 sts, SSK, K1; knit across instep (Needle 2) with no decreases; on Needle 3, K1, K2tog, K to end.

-Round 2: Work even (no decreases).

-Repeat rows 1 and 2 until the total of the heel stitches equals the number of instep stitches. You should know have a total of 20 (24, 28) stitches on your three needles.

AVOID THE GUSSET HOLE

Ask any sock knitter about the infamous "gusset hole" and you'll get a knowing nod and an eye-roll.

This happens when you pick up the stitches along the heel flap. You end up with a little hole in the top corner of the triangle. You can go back when your sock is finished and do a quick stitch on the inside of the sock to close up the hole, but why not avoid it altogether?

When you are picking up stitches for the heel to shape the gusset, try this. On each inside corner, where the heel flap meets the instep, pick up an extra stitch on the flap, along with the stitch *one row below* the first stitch on the instep. Then knit these two stitches together.

FOOT

Once you've finished the heel—the flap, the turn, the gusset—you can take it easy. Just knit around all of your stitches, with no decreases. When the foot of your sock (from where the heel flap meets the turn) is ***half an inch shorter*** than the desired length of the foot, you are ready to work the toe decreases and finish the sock.

SHAPE THE TOE

The toe is shaped on the outside edges, with decreases on each edge of the instep and the outside edge of the bottom stitches (Needles 1 and 3).

Decrease Round:

-Needle 1 (1st heel side): Knit to last 3 sts, SSK, K1.

-Needle 2 (instep): K1, K2tog, K to last 3 sts, SSK, K1.

-Needle 3 (2nd heel side): K1, K2tog, k to end

-Start the shaping by doing decreases every other round until you've got only 8 stitches remaining. Cut the working strand, leaving a six-inch tail. Thread it on a darning or tapestry needle. Weave the needle through the stitches on your double-pointed needles. Pull it tight—like a drawstring—to close up the hole. Weave the thread through the stitches on the inside to secure them. Weave in any other loose ends.

CHAPTER 5: BABY BLOSSOM HAT

This hat is so easy to knit and can be made in with any yarn that's suitable for a baby. Try a textured or variegated yarn for something different. Leave off the flower and this hat is great for boys, too!

Materials:

-80 yards of Worsted weight yarn (#4)

-8 yards of DK or Worsted for flower

-4 yards of DK or Worsted for leaves

-Size 7 double-pointed needles

Gauge:

-5 stitches = 1 inch on size 7

Finished Size:

	Newborn	3-6 month	6-12 months
Circumference	12" / 30.5cm	14" / 35.5cm	16" / 40.5cm
Height (includes 2" roll)	7.5" / 19cm	8.5" / 21.5cm	9.5" / 24cm

Abbreviations:

-K1 f&b: Knit 1 stitch, front and back. This step is used to create two stitches from one. Knit into the front of the stitch and then pull the needle through as if you are going to knit it, BUT then insert the needle into the back loop of the same stitch and finish the knit stitch.

-P1 f&b: Purl 1 stitch, front and back. This step is used to create two stitches from one. Purl into the next stitch and then pull the needle through the front as if you're going to purl it, BUT then pull that working needle up and over the stitch and insert the same needle into the back loop of the same stitch and finish the purl stitch.

-PSSO: Pass slipped stitch over. It is used following a slipped stitch, as if binding off.

HAT INSTRUCTIONS:

Instructions are given for Newborn, with 3-6 months and 6-12 months in parentheses.

-Cast on 60 (70, 80) stitches. Knit around and attach yarn to beginning stitch to close up gap.

-Continue knitting every round until piece measures 5.5" (6.5", 7.5"). NOTE: If you want the brim to roll more, keep knitting for another inch.

To work the crown, do the decrease rows as follows:

-Round 1: *Knit 8 st, K2TOG*; repeat from * to * to end of round—54 (63, 72) sts remaining.

-Round 2 and all even-numbered rounds: K.

-Round 3: *Knit 7 st, K2TOG*; repeat from * to * to end of round—48 (56, 64) sts remaining.

-Round 5: *Knit 6 st, K2TOG*; repeat from * to * to end of round—42 (49, 56) sts remaining.

-Round 7: *Knit 5 st, K2TOG*; repeat from * to * to end of round—36 (42, 48) sts remaining.

-Round 9: *Knit 4 st, K2TOG*; repeat from * to * to end of round—30 (35, 40) sts remaining.

-Round 11: *Knit 3 st, K2TOG*; repeat from * to * to end of round—24 (28, 32) sts remaining.

-Round 13: *Knit 2 st, K2TOG*; repeat from * to * to end of round—18 (21, 24) sts remaining.

-Round 15: *Knit 1 st, K2TOG*; repeat from * to * to end of round—12 (14, 16) sts remaining.

-Round 17: *K2TOG*; repeat from * to * to end of round—6 (7, 8) sts remaining.

-After Round 17, cut yarn, leaving a 6-inch tail. Thread the tail onto a darning needle and then weave the needle through the remaining stitches. Slide them off the needles and pull like a drawstring to close up the hole. Weave in the remainder of the tail.

ROSE INSTRUCTIONS:

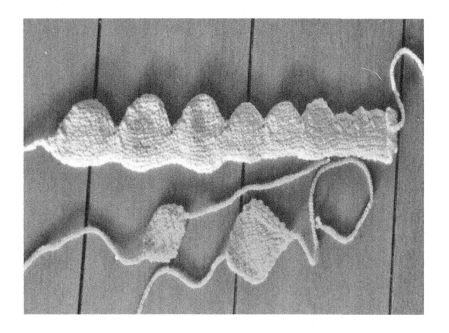

The rose is worked in one long strip and then rolled up. You'll start by making 4 small petals, and then 3 medium-sized petals, and 3 large petals, and they are all connected. It looks like a lot of instructions, but this is easy knitting that works up very fast.

-Cast on 5 st.

-Row 1: K1 f&b, K4—6 sts total.

-Row 2: P4, P1 f&b, P1—7 sts total.

-Row 3: K7.

-Row 4: P7.

-Row 5: K1, K2tog, K4—6 sts.

-Row 6: P3, P2tog, P1—5 sts total.

-Repeat Rows 1-6 three more times, so you'll end with 4 petals.

Now, you are going to proceed to knit the *medium petals* on the same strip, so don't cut your yarn; just keep knitting.

-Row 7: K1 f&b, K4—6 sts total.

-Row 8: P4, P1 f&b, P1—7 sts total.

-Row 9: K1 f&b, K6—8 sts total.

-Row 10: P6, P1 f&b, P1—9 sts total.

-Rows 11 and 13: K9.

-Rows 12 and 14: P9.

-Rows 15 and 17: K1, K2tog, K to end.

-Rows 16 and 18: P to last 3 sts; P2tog, P1. You should have 5 sts remaining at end of Row 18.

-Repeats Rows 7-18 two more times, so you've added 3 petals to the strip.

Next, you'll knit the *large petals* on the same strip, without cutting your yarn.

-Rows, 19, 21 and 23: K1 f&b, K to end.

-Rows 20, 22 and 24: P to last 2 sts; P1 f&b, P1. At end of Row 24, you should have 11 sts.

-Rows 25, 27 and 29: K11.

-Rows 26, 28 and 30: P11.

-Rows 31, 33 and 35: K1, K2tog, K to end.

-Rows 32, 34 and 36: P to last 3 sts; P2tog, P1. At end of Row 36, you should have 5 sts.

-Repeat Rows 19-36 two more times.

-Row 37: K1, K2tog, K2—4 sts remaining.

-Row 38: P1, P2tog, P1—3 sts.

-Row 39: K1, K2tog—2 sts.

-Row 40: P2tog. Cut tail and slip through last stitch. Tighten the strand to secure the knot.

-Press the petal strip. Starting from the small petal end, roll up the strip with the WRONG side facing outwards. Stitch the bottom edges together, so your rose does not unwind. Curl the petals outward.

Leaf Instructions:

You will make two leaves—a small and a big one.

-For the *large leaf*, cast on 3 st.

-Row 1 and all odd-numbered (Wrong Side) rows: P.

-Row 2 (RS): [K1 f&b] twice, K1—5 sts total.

-Row 4: [K1 f&b] twice, K3—7 sts total.

-Row 6: [K1 f&b] twice, K5—9 sts total.

-Row 8: [K1 f&b] twice, K7—11 sts total.

-Row 10: [K1 f&b] twice, K9—13 sts total.

-Row 12: K.

-Row 14: SSK, K9, K2tog—11 sts total.

-Row 16: SSK, K7, K2tog—9 sts total.

-Row 18: SSK, K5, K2tog—7 sts total.

-Row 20: SSK, K3, K2tog—5 sts total.

-Row 22: SSK, K1, K2tog—3 sts total.

-Row 24: Sl2, PSSO—1 st.

-Cut tail and slip through last stitch. Tighten the strand to secure the knot.

-For the *small leaf,* follow the same pattern, for Rows 1-7, OMIT Rows 8-15, and finish with Rows 16-24.

-Attach one tip of each leaf to the stitched base of the flower. Before attaching the flower to the hat, be sure to roll up the brim so that it is placed where it will be seen, and not inside the brim!

CHAPTER 6: LITTLE FISHERMAN'S HAT

This hat is a mini-version of the one worn by New England fisherman, although I chose blue instead of yellow for a particular boy in Maine.

Materials:

-50 yards of Bulky weight yarn (#5)

-Size 10 double pointed needles

Gauge:

-3 stitches = 1 inch

Finished Size:

	Newborn	3-6 month	6-12 months
Circumference at Forehead	12" / 30.5cm	14" / 35.5cm	16" / 40.5cm
Height (includes 3" brim in front)	8.5" / 19cm	9.5" / 21.5cm	10.5" / 24cm

Instructions:

Instructions are given for Newborn, with 3-6 months and 6-12 months in parentheses.

-Cast on 46 (52, 58) stitches). Divide them evenly among 3 dpns. Knit one round and join the yarn.

-Knit 5 rows for the edge of the brim.

-Round 1: Purl 23 (26, 29) sts, pm, P to end.

-Round 2: Purl to 3 sts before marker, P2tog, P1; slip marker, P1, P2tog, P to end of round—34 (40, 46) sts remaining.

-Round 3: P (no decreases).

-Repeat Rounds 2 and 3 until 36 (42, 48) sts remain.

-Knit evenly for 4 (5, 6) inches.

Decrease As Follows:

-Round 1: *Knit 4 st, K2TOG*; repeat from * to * to end of round—30 (35, 40) sts remaining.

-Round 2 and all eve-numbered rows: Knit evenly around (no decreases).

-Round 3: *Knit 3 st, K2TOG*; repeat from * to * to end of round—24 (28, 32) sts remaining.

-Round 5: *Knit 2 st, K2TOG*; repeat from * to * to end of round—18 (21, 24) sts remaining.

-Round 7: *Knit 1 st, K2TOG*; repeat from * to * to end of round—12 (14, 16) sts remaining.

-Round 9: *K2TOG*; repeat from * to * to end of round—6 (7, 8) sts remaining.

-After Round 9, cut yarn, leaving a 6-inch tail. Thread the tail onto a darning needle and then weave the needle through the remaining stitches. Slide them off the needles and pull like a drawstring to close up the hole. Weave in the remainder of the tail.

-Cut yarn, leaving a 6-inch tail. Thread the tail onto a darning needle and then weave the needle through the remaining stitches. Slide them off the needles and pull like a drawstring to close up the hole. Weave in the remainder of the tail.

-Tack the front of the brim to the hat, using the whip stitch.

I-Cord Chin Strap:

In order to keep the hat on an infant, you'll need a chin strap. You can add a piece of elastic or knit two I-cord pieces as follows.

-Cast on 3 sts on 1 dpn. Slide the stitches to the opposite end of the needles and knit them, starting with the stitch opposite the tail. Repeat this process until you have an 8-inch strap. Bind off, and knit a second strap. Secure each one inside the hat, at the point where the brim becomes the hat.

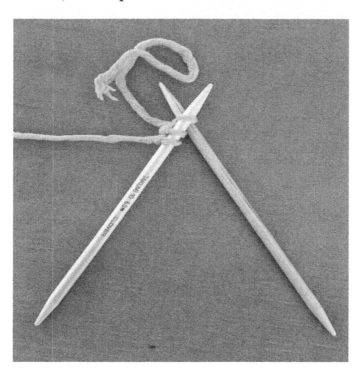

CHAPTER 7: LACY BLANKET

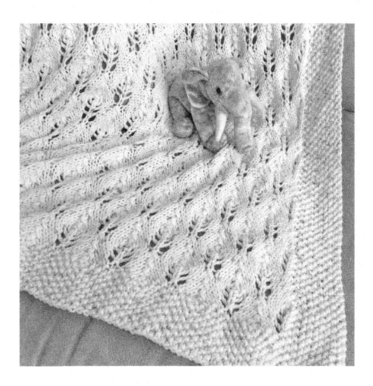

This blanket features a lacy pattern that looks complicated, but is very easy to knit. If you can do a yarnover (yo), you are all set!

Materials:

-1,100 yards of Worsted weight yarn (#4)

-Size 9 circular needles (at least 24" long)

Gauge:

-4 stitches = 1 inch

Finished Size:

-36" X 36"

Abbreviations:

-pm: Place stitch marker.

-yo: Yarnover. When knitting, bring the strand of working yarn to the front, between the two needles. When you knit the stitch, there's an extra wrap, which creates the eyelet holes in this pattern.

-PSSO: Pass slipped stitch over. It is used following a slipped stitch, as if binding off.

Seed Stitch Pattern:

-*K1, P1*; repeat from * to * across row. On every successive row, knit the purl stitch and purl the knit stitch.

Lacy Flame Stitch Pattern:

-Rows 1, 3, 5 and 7: K1, *yo, K3, sl1 K2tog, psso, K3, yo, K1*; repeat from * to * to end.

-Row 2 and all even-numbered rows: Purl.

-Rows 9, 11, 13 and 15: K2tog, K3, yo, K1, K3, *sl1 K2tog, psso, K3, yo, K1, yo, K3*; repeat from * to * to last 2 sts; end with sl1, K1, psso.

Instructions:

-Cast on 141 stitches.

-Work Seed Stitch for 14 rows.

-Row 1: Continue seed stitch for first 10 stitches; pm; work Row 1 of Lacy Flames pattern stitch until 10 stitches remain; pm; continue working last 10 sts in Seed Stitch pattern.

-Continue in this pattern, working the first and last 10 stitches of each row in Seed Stitch, and the 121 stitches in the middle in the Lacy Flame Stitch.

-Repeat pattern until blanket measures 34" from the cast on. Work Seed Stitch across entire row for 14 rows. Bind off.

CHAPTER 8: COLOR BLOCKED CARDIGAN

This pattern is for a basic baby cardigan. I used a variegated yarn for the body and sleeves, with contrast for the ribbing. You can add contrasting colors wherever you like, by using even more colors than I have here. Change up the color on each of the front panels. Use different colors for the ribbing.

Materials:

-240 yards of Worsted weight yarn (#4) for body and sleeves (Main Color = MC)

-80 yards of Worsted weight yarn for ribbing (Contrasting Color = CC)

-Size 8 straight or circular needles

-6 buttons

-3 stitch holders

Gauge:

-5 stitches = 1 inch

Finished Size:

-Pattern is written for 6-month size; instructions for 12 and months are in parentheses. See page 11 for Size Chart.

Instructions:

Back

-In CC, cast on 28 (32, 36) sts. K2, P2 rib for 9 rows, increasing 4 sts evenly across last row—32 (36, 40).

-Change to MC. Work in stockinette until piece measures 5.5" (6.5", 7.5").

Shape Armhole

-Rows 1 and 2: Bind off 2 (2, 3) sts at the beginning of the row; work in stockinette to end.

-Rows 3 and 4: Bind off 1 st at beginning of row; work in stockinette to end—26 (30, 32). Work even in stockinette until back measures 10" (11", 12"). Place the stitches on a stitch holder and set aside while you work the two front pieces.

Left Front:

-In CC, cast on 16 (18, 20) sts. K2, P2 rib for 9 rows.

-Change to MC. Work in stockinette until piece measures 5.5" (6.5", 7.5").

Shape Armhole:

-Row 1: Bind off 2 (2, 3) sts at the beginning of the row, K across.

-Row 2: P.

-Row 3: Bind off 1 (1, 1) st at the beginning of the row, K across—13 (15, 16) sts.

-Continue in stockinette until piece measures 8" (9", 10"), ending at the *start of a purl row*.

Shape Neck:

-Row 1: Bind off 4 sts at the beginning of the row, P across.

-Row 2: K to last 3 sts; end with K2tog, K1.

-Row 3: P1, P2tog, P to end.

-Repeat Rows 2 and 3 until 9 sts remain. Work evenly until piece measures 10" (11", 12"). Place the stitches on a stitch holder.

Right Front:

-In CC, cast on 16 (18, 20) sts. K2, P2 rib for 9 rows.

-Change to MC. Work in stockinette until piece measures 5.5" (6.5", 7.5").

Shape Armhole:

-Row 1: On the purl side, bind off 2 (2, 3) sts at the beginning of the row, P across.

-Row 2: K.

-Row 3: Bind off 1 (1, 1) st at the beginning of the row, P across—13 (15, 16) sts.

-Continue in stockinette until piece measures 8" (9", 10"), ending at the *start of a knit row*.

Shape Neck:

-Row 1: Bind off 4 sts at the beginning of the row, K across.

-Row 2: P to last 3 sts; end with P2tog, P1.

-Row 3: K1, K2tog, K to end.

-Repeat Rows 2 and 3 until 9 sts remain. Work evenly until piece measures 10" (11", 12"). Place the stitches on a stitch holder.

Attach Back To Front At Shoulders:

-With right sides facing one another, line up the shoulder seam on the front with the back. Do a three-needle bind-off as follows:

-Holding the two needles parallel to one another in your left hand, insert a third needle into the first stitch on each of the two needles. Knit them together.

-Repeat this step with the second stitch. Then, bind off as you normally would, passing the slipped stitch over. Continue until the 9 stitches for the front have been bound off,

-Repeat this step for the opposite shoulder. Leave the remaining 8 (12, 14) sts on the holder to work for the neck.

Sleeves:

-With MC, pick up 34 sts across the armhole edge of the sweater. Work in stockinette for 4 rows. The decrease as follows:

-Row 1 and 3: K1, SSK, K to last 3 sts, K2tog, K1.

-Row 2 and all even-numbered rows: P.

-Repeat Rows 1-4 seven times—20 sts remaining.

-Work evenly until sleeve measures 5" (6", 6.5").

-Change to CC. Work in K2, P2 rib for 9 rows. Bind off.

-Stitch side seams, from wrist to waist.

Add Ribbing To Left Front:

-With the right side of the sweater facing you, pick up and knit 44 stitches along the left front edge. Work in K2, P2 rib for 9 rows. Bind off loosely.

-ADD RIBBING TO RIGHT FRONT (WITH BUTTONHOLES)

-With the right side of the sweater facing you, pick up and knit 44 stitches along the right front edge. Work in K2, P2 rib for 3 rows.

-To make the buttonholes, continue working in the rib, BUT after the fourth stitch in the row, bind off two stitches. Keeping in the K2, P2 pattern, repeat the two-stitch bind-off after every 7 stitches. You should end up with 5 buttonholes.

-In the next row, continue in the rib pattern. When you come to the bound-off stitches, cast on 2 stitches to close the gap.

-Work 4 more rows in the rib and bind off loosely.

Add Ribbing To Neck:

-Starting from the front left neck edge, pick up and knit 18 (20, 22) stitches, then the remaining 8 (12, 14) sts from the holder on the back neck. Pick up 18 (20, 22) stitches along the right front edge—44 (52, 58) sts.

-Work in K2, P2 rib for 2 rows. Make a 6th buttonhole on the right front of the neck as follows: Work the first 3 stitches from the edge, bind off 2, and continue in K2, P2 pattern. On the next row, cast on 2 stitches to replace the ones you have bound off. Continue in the rib pattern for 5 more rows and bind off loosely.

Assembly:

-Line up the buttons with the buttonholes and stitch the buttons to the ribbing. Weave in all loose ends.

-Remember: When you block the sweater, do not press the ribbing or you'll lose the elastic effect of it.

KNITTING TERMS GLOSSARY

Knitters have a language all their own. As you move beyond this book, you will encounter books and patterns that use a variety of standard abbreviations. Here's a list of what you will need to know in order to understand the instructions.

* *: Repeat the instructions between the two asterisks.

-Alt: alternate (as in "alt rows").

-Beg: beginning

-Bet: between

-BO: bind off

-CA: color A (when you are using more than one color)

-CB: color B (see above)

-CC: contrasting color (ditto!)

-Cn: cable needle, which could be either a small hook or something that looks like an overgrown toothpick with a curve in the middle, used to holding stitches when making a cable stitch

-Cont: continue

-Dec: decrease

-DK: double knitting; a yarn weight or knitting technique

-Dp, dpn: double-pointed needle

-EON: end of needle

-EOR: end of row

-Fl: front loop

-Foll: follow or following

-G st: garter stitch (knitting every row)

-Incl: including

-K: knit

-K tbl: knit through back loop, which creates a twist on the finished stitch

-K1 f&b: knit into the front of the stitch and then into the back of the same stitch

-K2tog: knit two stitches together

-K2tog tbl: knit two stitches together through the back loop instead of the front

-LC: left cross, a cable stitch where the front of the cross slants to the left

-LH: left hand

-Lp: loop

-LT: left twist, a stitch that creates a mock cable slanted to the left

-M1: Make 1 stitch, which requires an increase method

-MC: main color

-P: purl

-P tbl: purl through the back loop instead of the front

-P up: pick up

-P2tog: purl two stitches together

-P2tog tbl: purl two stitches together through the back loop instead of the front

-Patt: pattern

-Pm: place stitch marker

-Prev: previous

-Psso: pass slipped stitch over (as in binding off)

-Pu: pick up (stitches)

-RC: right cross, a cable stitch where the front of the cross slants to the right

-Rem: remaining

-Rep: repeat

-RH: right hand

-Rnd: round(s); when knitting on a circular or double pointed needle when the yarn is joined, you knit in rounds, not rows

-RS: right side

-RT: right twist, a stitch that creates a mock cable slanted to the right

-Sk: skip

-Sk2p: slip 1 stitch, knit 2 together, and then pass the slipped stitch over the knitted ones to create a double decrease

-Skp: slip 1 stitch, knit 1 stitch, and then pass the slipped stitch over the knitted one to create a single decrease

-Sl, slst, slip: slip or slide a stitch without working it

-Sl, k1, psso: same as "skp"

-Sl1k: slip 1 stitch knit-wise

-Sl1p: slip 1 stitch purl-wise

-Ssk: slip 1 stitch, slip the next stitch, and then knit the 2 stitches together to create a left-slanting decrease

-Ssp: slip 1 stitch, slip the next stitch, and then purl the 2 stitches together to create a right-slanting decrease

-Sssk: slip 1 stitch, slip the next stitch, slip the 3rd and then knit the 3 stitches together to create a double, left-slanting decrease

-St: stitch

-Sts: stitches

-St st: stockinette stitch; alternately knit a row and purl a row

-Tbl: through the back loop (of a stitch)

-Tog: together

-WS: wrong side

-Wyib: with yarn in back

-Wyif: with yarn in front

-Yfwd: yarn forward (same as yarn over)

-Yo: yarn over, move yarn to the opposite direction

-Yrn: yarn 'round needle (same as yarn over)

Printed in Great Britain
by Amazon

40620508R00064